10 CHRISTMAS VOL. 4

CONTENTS

- ANGELS FROM THE REALM OF GLORY

- COVENTRY CAROL

- GESU BAMBINO

- GOOD CHRISTIAN MEN REJOICE

- LO, HOW A ROSE E'ER BLOOMING

- O TANNENBAUM (O CHRISTMAS TREE)

- THE HOLLY AND THE IVY

- UP ON THE HOUSETOP

- WASSAIL SONG

- WHILE SHEPHERDS WATCHED

ARRANGEMENTS BY B. C. DOCKERY ©2022

Angels From the Realm of Glory

Score

Henry Smart
B. C. Dockery

Angels From the Realm of Glory

Angels From the Realm of Glory

Cello I

Henry Smart
B. C. Dockery

Arr. ©2022

Angels From the Realm of Glory

Cello II

Henry Smart
B. C. Dockery

Angels From the Realm of Glory

Piano

Henry Smart
B. C. Dockery

Coventry Carol

Score

Traditional
B. C. Dockery

Arr. ©2022

Coventry Carol

Cello 1

Traditional
B. C. Dockery

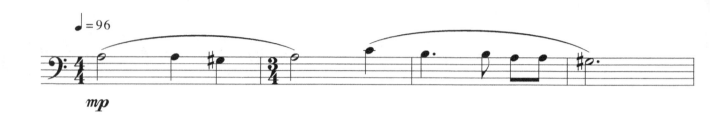

Arr. ©2022

Coventry Carol

Cello 2

Traditional
B. C. Dockery

Arr. ©2022

Coventry Carol

Piano

Traditional
B. C. Dockery

Gesu Bambino

Score

Pietro Yon
B. C. Dockery

Arr. ©2022

Gesu Bambino

Cello I

Pietro Yon
B. C. Dockery

Gesu Bambino

Cello II

Pietro Yon
B. C. Dockery

Arr. ©2022

Gesu Bambino

Piano

Pietro Yon
B. C. Dockery

Good Christian Men, Rejoice!

Score

Traditional German
B. C. Dockery

Arr. ©2022

Good Christian Men, Rejoice!

Good Christian Men, Rejoice!

Cello I

Traditional German
B. C. Dockery

Good Christian Men, Rejoice!

Cello II

Traditional German
B. C. Dockery

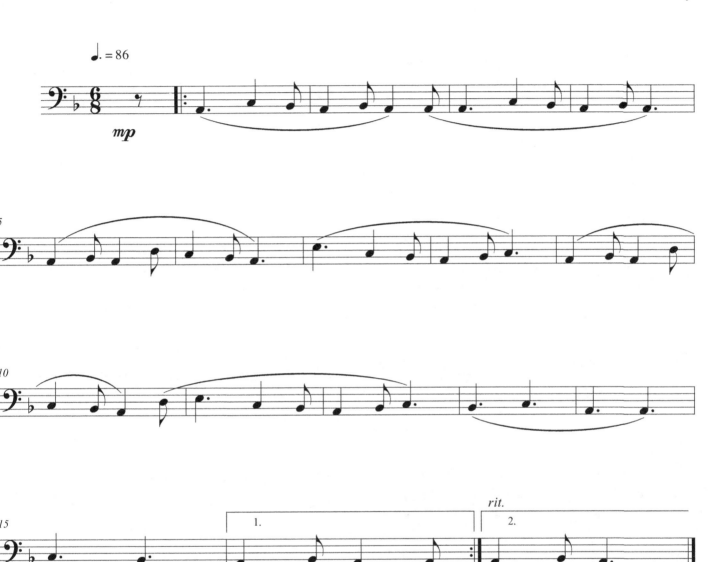

Good Christian Men, Rejoice!

Piano

Traditional German
B. C. Dockery

Lo, How a Rose E'er Blooming

Score

Traditional
B. C. Dockery

Arr. ©2022

Lo, How a Rose E'er Blooming

Cello 1

Traditional
B. C. Dockery

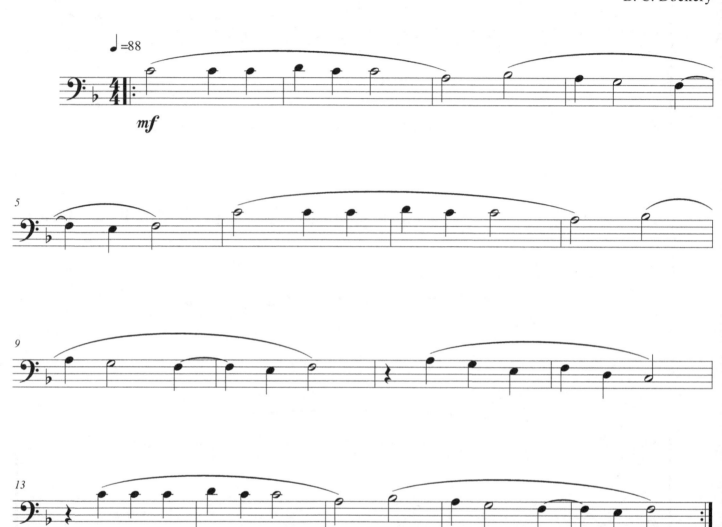

Lo, How a Rose E'er Blooming

Cello 2

Traditional
B. C. Dockery

Arr. ©2022

Lo, How a Rose E'er Blooming

Piano

Traditional
B. C. Dockery

O Christmas Tree

O Tannenbaum

Score

Traditional German
B. C. Dockery

Arr. ©2022

O Christmas Tree

O Christmas Tree

O Tannenbaum

Cello I

Traditional German
B. C. Dockery

O Christmas Tree

O Tannenbaum

Cello II

Traditional German
B. C. Dockery

Arr. ©2022

O Christmas Tree
O Tannenbaum

Piano

Traditional German
B. C. Dockery

The Holly and the Ivy

Score

Traditional English
B. C. Dockery

Arr. ©2022

The Holly and the Ivy

The Holly and the Ivy

Cello 1

Traditional English
B. C. Dockery

The Holly and the Ivy

Cello 2

Traditional English
B. C. Dockery

The Holly and the Ivy

Piano

Traditional English
B. C. Dockery

Up on the Housetop

Score

Benjamin Hanby
B. C. Dockery

Up on the Housetop

Cello 1

Benjamin Hanby
B. C. Dockery

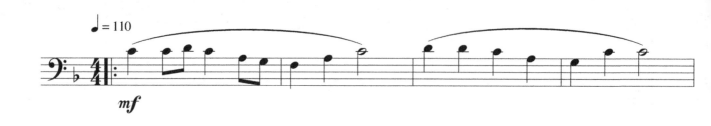

Up on the Housetop

Cello 2

Benjamin Hanby
B. C. Dockery

Arr. ©2022

Up on the Housetop

Piano

Benjamin Hanby
B. C. Dockery

Here We Come A-Caroling

Wassail Song

Score

Traditional English
B. C. Dockery

Arr. ©2022

Here We Come A-Caroling

Wassail Song

Cello I

Traditional English
B. C. Dockery

Here We Come A-Caroling

Wassail Song

Cello II

Traditional English
B. C. Dockery

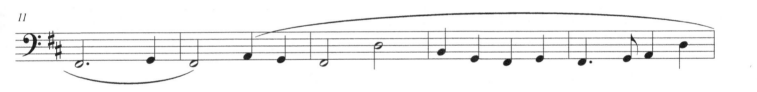

Arr. ©2022

Here We Come A-Caroling

Wassail Song

Piano

Traditional English
B. C. Dockery

Arr. ©2022

While Shepherds Watched Their Flock

Score

Nahum Tate
B. C. Dockery

While Shepherds Watched Their Flock

Cello 1

Nahum Tate
B. C. Dockery

While Shepherds Watched Their Flock

Cello 2

Nahum Tate
B. C. Dockery

While Shepherds Watched Their Flock

Piano

Nahum Tate
B. C. Dockery

Made in the USA
Las Vegas, NV
07 November 2023

80421781R00037